INOFFICIAL B[illegible]
INTERESTING FACTS
FOR
FORTNITE
FANS

Luprion

OUR PROMISE

Should there be any problems with the order,
the product arrives damaged or you are not satisfied with the product, then contact us within 30 days of ordering and we will refund your purchase.

We are 100% committed to our products and want to ensure your satisfaction with the product.

EXPECTATIONS FULFILLED?

Are you satisfied with the product?
Then we would be delighted if you would let us know what you think by leaving a review on Amazon. Even a single sentence is welcome.
This way you can help other customers with their purchase decision.
We also look forward to your personal message. Just write to us at:

kontakt@luprion.com

CONTENTS OF THIS BOOK

We regularly check the contents of this book to ensure that they are up to date. Nevertheless, incorrect information can sometimes creep in. If you notice something like this, you are welcome to point it out to us directly; see the email address above.

FOREWORD

Anyone who has ever immersed themselves in the world of Fortnite knows how exciting and complex this game can be. There is so much to discover, learn, and master: new maps, crazy dances, and, of course, the epic victory. But sometimes it's good to take a little break and move on to something else - something that doesn't necessarily contribute to success in the game, but is still entertaining nonetheless.

That's exactly why we wrote this book. It's a collection of useless knowledge about Fortnite facts that may not be vital to earning a win, but can still surprise, amuse, and maybe even trigger an aha! moment or two.

Think of it as a little break from Battle Royale, an opportunity to view the game from a new perspective, and maybe even expand your knowledge. Because even the seemingly useless can have its own appeal and become enriching.

This book does not claim to be a guide or how-to manual for Fortnite. Rather, it's an invitation to sit back, relax, and explore the world of Fortnite in a new, light-hearted way.

We hope you enjoy reading this book as much as we enjoyed writing it. Dive into the world of useless knowledge and let yourself be surprised!

NOT JUST A BIG MOUTH

RockyNoHands is a Fortnite player with a fantastic story to tell. Despite being completely paralyzed in both arms and legs after a fall, he hasn't let that stop him from pursuing his passion for the game. Using a QuadStick mouth joystick, which he operates with his mouth, he trained for years, and his perseverance and dedication eventually paid off. In March 2019, RockyNoHands achieved a remarkable milestone, celebrating his 509th victory in Battle Royale mode; a feat he achieved solely with this sophisticated mouth control system.

But RockyNoHands didn't stop there. In 2023, he even managed to eliminate 14 opponents in a battle royale. In doing so, he surpassed his own previous record of 11.

A "QuadStick" is a special type of joystick that is operated primarily by the mouth. It was developed to enable people with limited hand function to play video games. The controller works by blowing or sucking through an integrated straw. In addition, the QuadStick has sensors that detect lip movements.

PATIENCE IS A VIRTUE

Brandon Sanderson, author of the Mistborn series, commented on Reddit that collaborations, i.e. crossovers of other media outside the Fortnite brand that are introduced into the game, usually take 5 to 6 months to complete. The Cosmere Castaway Set was a prime example and was released on time after 5 months. But sometimes it does take longer, like with the Pac-Man set and the Galaxian emote. They had already reserved their IDs in August 2021, but then took a whole 10 months before they were finally released in June of the following year. Patience is not only a virtue when writing novels!

EYE YOGA

In the world of video games and films, strange errors can sometimes occur that make for bizarre moments. This once happened to the characters Vi and Sarah Connor, whose faces were briefly unnaturally deformed by a glitch, causing their eyes to bulge out when they danced.

SPAWN ISLAND TOURISM

Who says the fun in Fortnite has to end at the edges of the map? Daring players have transformed what was once an unreachable spawn island into a new destination for creative exploration. From daring bridge constructions to high-speed vehicle maneuvers, players developed a wide variety of methods to reach it.

Some of the most popular tricks included:

Bridge building and high-speed shopping cart rides - Acrobatic players built a bridge from the map to the spawn island and then used a shopping cart to dash across the structure at high speed.

Turbo boost with the Whiplash - Advanced builders also constructed a bridge, but this time they drove over it with a fully fueled Whiplash. The vehicle's boost enabled them to cover the distance in record time.

Flying with Choppa or Saucer - For the very brave, Choppa or Saucer offered a means of transportation. Although this method was riskier, as the vehicles could easily be shot down, it also enabled the fastest arrival.

The curious interaction of Shopping cart and minigun

You used to be able to race around Fortnite with a shopping cart and a minigun to mow everything down. You shot the minigun and moved in the opposite direction at the same time.

EPIC GAMES DEFIES GOOGLE PLAY

In August 2018, Fortnite was the talk of the town. But anyone searching for the battle royale hit in the Google Play Store received a surprising message: "Fortnite Battle Royale by Epic Games Inc is not available in the Google Play Store." Instead, the download link to competitor PUBG was displayed.

Why was this? Quite simply: money. Epic Games did not want to pay the fee that Google collects for all in-app purchases in the Play Store. So they simply offered Fortnite directly on their own website.

GAMBLE UNTIL YOUR EYES ARE SQUARE

Would you play Fortnite for 698 days in a row? That's how much time the player primesalad spent in the game until May 2024. That's an incredible 1,005,000 minutes. Imagine waking up every day, eating, maybe sleeping for a few hours and then playing Fortnite again. Day after day, for two years. To put that in perspective: Even if you're an avid Fortnite player and put four hours into the game every day, it would still take you 11.47 years to get the same amount of playtime as primesalad. That shows how much time and dedication he has put into Fortnite.

FROM FORTNITE FAME TO INSTA SHAME

Did you catch that Drake set Twitch ablaze in March 2018 when over 600,000 people watched him play Fortnite with streamer Tyler Ninja Blevins? However, this gaming bromance came to an end when Drake unfollowed Ninja on Instagram. The reason? Ninja had commented during a stream that Drake was probably just playing with him to gain more viewers. Drake is known for quickly unfollowing people when they talk about him publicly. Drake also owes Ninja 5,000 dollars for a Fortnite match.

THE MAGIC CARD

Did you know that the card that you throw into the air in the Card Drop emote remains on the ground for a few seconds before it disappears? Even if you use the emote again, the old card disappears first.

NOAH DECRYPTED

You're probably familiar with the popular "NOAH position" on the Fortnite map Apollo, right? If not, take a closer look at the area from the east. The path to Holly House forms an "N." A circle of hedges marks the

"O." The garden itself symbolizes the "A." And finally, the house stands for the "H."

It's as simple as that, the arrangement of these elements on the map results in the name "NOAH."

THE STAR FIGURE FROM LEGO FORTNITE

Brite Bomber is the most famous outfit used in advertising for LEGO Fortnite. She was the first character to appear in the very first reveal trailer.

SPIDER-MAN FANS TAKE NOTE

The 2099 Web Cape Back Bling is inspired by the first meeting of Miguel and Gwen in "Spider-Man: Across the Spider-Verse" and pays homage to the costume of his comic book counterpart.

WHEN YOUR OUTFIT BECOMES A DANCE BRAKE

You've probably been there too: you get dressed up, put on your smartest outfit, want to dance the night away and then you realize that you can hardly move. The collar is too tight, the sleeves too stiff, the pants too tight. Every movement seems cramped and unnatural. Players feel the same way when they choose certain outfits like Peely or Spacefarer Ariana Grande, which may look stylish but restrict their freedom of movement. If they then try to pull off a cool Head Banger, it looks more like a wobbly dachshund on the dashboard than a real head banger. The head jerks and jerks as if it doesn't really know what to do with itself.

VORTEX WITH DANCE SOUNDS

The Fortnite emote "Dance Moves" is more than just a collection of moves; it has a few musical secrets up its sleeve. You can choose between rocking electric guitar sounds and powerful marching drums. But watch out: The marching drum version only rocks on PC, Playstation, Xbox and the latest consoles it stays quiet on your Switch or cell phone.

FROM FAT TO FIT

Peter Griffin's muscular physique in Fortnite, which is very different from his usual stature, could be a hidden reference to an episode of Family Guy in which he undergoes liposuction. Family Guy creator Seth Macfarlane joked that Epic Games couldn't portray Peter's original physique due to budget constraints. However, the water fountain in Snooty Steppes features a statue of Peter Griffin in his original body, disproving Macfarlane's statement.

SAMSUNG TRICKED

To unlock the Galaxy Outfit, you had to play three Fortnite rounds on a Galaxy Note 9 or Tab S2. So instead of forking out the hefty sum of over 1,000 euros for the smartphone at the time, some players took advantage of the opportunity. They visited electronics stores to install Fortnite on the freely available demonstration devices and play the required three rounds to unlock the coveted skin.

But this trick was not without risk. In addition to the threat of being kicked out of the store, the players also risked exposing their sensitive account data. After all, using public devices always carries the risk of personal information falling into the wrong hands.

Samsung, understandably not happy about this creative circumvention of the actual incentive to buy, reacted promptly and blocked downloads on the demonstration devices. But the players, driven by their desire for the exclusive skin, were not discouraged. They found ways to circumvent the block; for example, by setting up a personal hotspot with their own smartphone to bypass the store's blocked Wi-Fi.

Real 5-Heads!

SHORT AND SWEET

The emote's name, "Keep it Mello," is a direct reference to the song of the same name by electronic music producer Marshmello and rapper Omar LinX.

Ahsoka Tano was the final outfit in the Star Wars series in Chapter 4 of *Fortnite*.

If a player wore the Camille Outfit during the Fracture event, Ava was shown her place on the screen during downtime.

The saucer's energy projectiles ricochet harmlessly off the beach umbrellas.

SHORT AND SWEET

The "Friendly Finger" Emote is an allusion to the fist bump gesture from the American sitcom "Friends," which is synonymous with the middle finger in the series.

Some burst-fire weapons used to have a bug in their rate of fire when used by AIs. This caused them to fire very quickly, as if they were fully automatic weapons.

The Back Bling "Auto Clutch" is a redesigned version of the Haute Holster.

On the map "Apollo," at the bottom of the Sharky Shell, there is a clear echo that can be heard when the player does something that causes noise.

HEROES NICKNAMES FOR TAKER

In the military, code names are often used for operations or enemy units in order to communicate quickly and efficiently. It's similar in Fortnite, where the Taker is referred to differently depending on which hero you play. Jonesy, for example, calls them "dive bombers", while Ken refers to them as "soul suckers". Thunder Thora, on the other hand, has opted for the nickname "flying husks."

LEGO BREAKS RECORDS

The new LEGO mode in *Fortnite* has cracked the 2.4 million player mark in just two days. And that's despite the fact that you don't fight each other, but build and survive together in a Minecraft-like world. Even the absolute player record was broken: Over 2.4 million players were active in LEGO mode at the same time, while the other modes together only counted 1.9 million players.

FROM INTERNAL FUN TO SUCCESS

Following the release of "Gears of War 3" in 2011, a creative atmosphere prevailed at Epic Games. An inhouse game jam allowed the developers to freely express their ideas. Although Fortnite was not directly created during this event, the foundation for the concept was laid here: What if you could combine the building mechanics of games like Minecraft or Terraria with the action-packed elements of a shooter? This visionary question soon became reality: Fortnite took shape and transformed from an inhouse fun project into a global success.

A "game jam" is an event in which the participants attempt to completely redevelop a video game within a certain period of time. The duration of the game jam varies depending on the format and is usually between 24 and 72 hours. Participants can either work independently or in teams. Typically, programmers, game designers, artists, authors and other people involved in game development take part in a game jam.

FINALLY SOMEONE YOU CAN TALK TO

You visit a foreign country, want to talk to the locals and have to communicate with your hands and feet. But imagine traveling to an ancient empire, meeting the Queen of the Ruins and she speaks your native language fluently! No more tedious translating, no more guesswork. Just a relaxed conversation with the ruler about times gone by and her secrets. Sounds like a dream, right? But in *Fortnite*, this became reality. Queen Orelia is currently the only boss who can speak your chosen language.

GHOST STONES ARE SOMETIMES HAUNTED

Did you know that the Shadow Stones in Fortnite have a pretty buggy past? They were deactivated a total of four times or had bugs when they were introduced. The item had to be removed from the game twice. In addition, a bug allowed players to use their Harvesting Tool even though they were actually invisible ghosts.

FROM ANOMALIES TO ANARCHY

Remember the Sideways Anomalies? The players who entered them suffered from extremely high latency, resulting in unplayable stutters and delays. But that wasn't all. After leaving the anomalies, many players had problems moving normally and were pulled back uncontrollably. Epic intervened and temporarily removed them from the game.

„Sideways Anomalies" were special zones that appeared randomly on the map. These zones had a distinct visual change, creating a bubble-like area with a purple glow and low gravity. Inside, players encountered unique enemies and could find special loot that only existed in these anomalies.

CLIX CONQUERS THE TWITCH THRONE

With 2.76 million viewer hours in the past 30 days on Twitch, Clix was the most popular Fortnite streamer in January 2024. The young pro wowed his audience with his exceptional skills, exciting moves and positive attitude.

DURRR BURGER IN THE REAL WORLD

In the summer of 2018, a giant statue suddenly appeared in the middle of the Californian desert. It looked like the Durrr Burger from Fortnite. As it later turned out, this surprise was part of a promotional campaign by Epic Games.

HOLY MACKEREL

An early design of the Batman Zero Wing, which was based on the Batglider from Batman: Arkham Knight and hinted at the „No Confidence" storyline, was accidentally leaked on the DC Comics website a month before the official release.

Oops!

DON'T FIX WHAT ISN'T BROKEN

Are you getting on with the built-in aim assist so far? Many Save the World players are calling for the changes to Battle Royale's aim assist not to be applied to Save the World, as many find it difficult to hit the Husks.

AS SOON AS YOU SWITCH ON THE CAR RADIO IN THE BATTLE BUS, THE LIGHTS IN THE BUS COME TO LIFE AND CONJURE UP A REAL DISCO ATMOSPHERE, AS IF A SPARKLING DISCO BALL WERE FLOATING INSIDE. EVEN THE BUS'S HORN GETS A NEW, COOL SOUND WHEN THE MUSIC IS BLARING.

BECAUSE YOUR EGO DESERVES A SWORD TOO

The Blade of Ages Pickaxe, which was introduced in Chapter 5: Season 2, displays an emblem on its hilt in Ranked that corresponds to your current rank. Whether bronze, silver, gold, platinum or champion the Blade of Ages lets your opponents know at a glance who they are up against in a ranked match.

MINECRAFT MEETS TOWER DEFENSE

Have you ever noticed how much Fortnite has changed over the years? When the game was announced in 2011, it was a far cry from the battle royale phenomenon we know today. Back then, Fortnite was described by journalists as a mixture of Minecraft and Tower Defense. Can you imagine what it might have looked like? Towers instead of walls, creepers instead of opponents - a pretty bizarre idea!

CONTROLLER INSTEAD OF KEYBOARD

Do you play on a console yourself? Then you belong to the majority, because 78% of Fortnite players also play on a console. Fortnite runs on Xbox, PlayStation, Mac, PC and even Nintendo Switch and many Android pho- nes. PC and Mac support all game modes, while conso- les lack a few extras. Fortnite is particularly successful on the PlayStation 4, which generates almost half of all revenue, followed by the Xbox One.

FORTNITE'S ALMOST EARLY END

Development problems and delays in 2012 drove the then-director of Epic Games, Rod Fergusson, to the brink of despair. In this situation, he even considered putting the ambitious project on ice altogether and abandoning it. Fortunately for Fortnite fans, the final decision turned out differently. The decision was made to continue on the chosen path despite all the adversity. Although Fergusson left Epic Games in 2012, development of the game continued.

LOST IN TIME

The "Endless Ned" Outfit is a tribute to a unique character called Ned from Fortnite: Save the World. In the quest line "The Long Road Home," you meet Ned, who only wants to be rescued once you have found a med kit for him. During the quest series, it was discovered that he was always present when someone was manipulating time. As a result, he was caught in a time loop and thrown uncontrollably through various points in time.

THE POWER AWAKENS

The first Star Wars outfits to make the Fortnite galaxy unsafe since Chapter 4 were: Anakin Skywalker, Padmé Amidala, Darth Maul, 212th Battalion Trooper, 501st Trooper, Wolf Pack Trooper, Ahsoka's Clone Trooper and Coruscant Guard.

FROM TAMAGOTCHI TO TOP-LOOT

Have you ever wondered where the inspiration for the cuddly 8-bit Champions Back Bling came from? They are a tribute to the iconic Tamagotchi. This Japanese electronic toy, whose name is made up of the words "tamago" (egg) and "wottchi" (watch), took the world by storm in 1997.

FORTNITE'S BOUNCIEST BOOTH

Have you already experienced it? In Fortnite, an Outfit Booth can throw you back if another player is in it. If you stand too close to the occupied booth, it acts like a magnet and you fly through the air. So it's better to keep your distance if you don't want to suddenly perform an unintentional aerial acrobatic feat. Then crash your car in front of the Outfit Booth instead? Not a good idea either. You will also be thrown back or the vehicle will be completely destroyed. The player leaving the Outfit Booth will not be injured.

MULTIVERSAL IDENTITY CRISIS

To explain the different personalities and appearances of characters who are actually the same person (e.g. Slurp Jonesy and Bunker Jonesy), there is the idea of "Snapshots". These Snapshots can be thought of as different versions of the same character from different points in time or realities. For example, Slurp Jonesy may have become a heroic protector in one reality, while Bunker Jonesy is a grim survivor in another.

SAFE CRACKING FOR PROFESSIONALS

You discover a gigantic vault filled to the brim with legendary weapons and equipment. But even in the virtual world of Fortnite, the laws of physics apply. This colossus is not only heavy, but also reacts to gravity. If you blow up the ground beneath it, it will plummet into the depths or slide down the slope. You can even push and move it with vehicles. But be careful, the safe is very robust and has 500 health points. So, grab your best tool and crack the thing.

THERE SHOULD BE A RECOUNT

Anyone who has been playing Fortnite for any length of time is sure to have experienced the odd glitch or bug. But this one stands out in particular, because it could rob you of your well-earned cheers: there was a bug with the "Crowning Achievement" Emote that caused the counter to drop to 00 when you reached 100 victories. However, the bug has since been fixed and the counter can now still track over 1000 victories.

Next time you see an opponent with 0 victories, you can spam the Take The L Emote with a clear conscience ;)

FAMILY GUY‘S CRAZY CLIP SHOW COLLECTION

Have you noticed that the Clip Show Carry-All Back Bling presents some moments from the series "Family Guy"? Examples include: In "In the Frenzy of Music," Peter Griffin holds his knee in pain. In "Three's Too Many," the Petercopter's leaves spin in Joe Swanson's garden. In "Everybody Loves Jesus," Brian Griffin watches Peter Griffin dance to the second half of Surfin Bird after getting up.

#KEVINFORPRESIDENT

Did you know that fans have affectionately christened the purple cube in Fortnite "Kevin"? Sounds funny, doesn't it? But there's a reason for it: In a Reddit thread, the word "cube" was banned, so fans had to get creative and gave it the name "Kevin" without further ado.

APOLLO'S EXTREME TOUR

You know the map "Apollo," but have you ever wondered which is the highest and lowest point on the map? Well, as you maneuvered your way through the canyons of Apollo, the majestic Mount Kay in grid G7 was the highest point you could reach. Recognizable by its proud flagpole, it towered over Catty Corner and the Fortnite weather station. The lowest point, on the other hand, is the mysterious Coral Castle. Hidden in the northwest corner of the island, it was originally an underwater kingdom that only came to light when the sea level dropped. Every step you took there was literally the deepest point you could reach in Apollo.

CLOTHES MAKE THE MAN

There was a bug where the preview of the Suit Up Emote preview on the Battle Pass screen of your currently equipped outfit instead of Tony Stark was displayed. This could cause the original textures of outfits based on others, become visible.

LEGO MINIGUN FROM FORTNITE

Who doesn't know it? The legendary minigun from Fortnite, which is feared in the game for its destructive power. For LEGO fans and Fortnite enthusiasts alike, a dream came true when LEGO designer and YouTuber "Nombies" presented a replica of the minigun in February 2018. This construction made from over 6,000 LEGO bricks is not only an eye-catcher, but also a real colossus: with a length of 140 cm and a weight of over 8 kg, the LEGO minigun clearly surpasses its game model. Nombies invested 60 hours in the construction of the detailed replica. The result of his work is impressive: The minigun can be rotated, has movable barrels and a detachable magazine.

A.I.M.'S MOST EMBARRASSING PHASE

The A.I.M. Outfit, which looks like a robot, originally looked very different. According to Drew Hill, one of the developers, green pants and untracked feet were planned for the character. However, these designs were later adapted to better suit A.I.M.'s background story.

THE CREEPING CAT

You know how it is: if you want to sneak up on someone in real life, you have to move like a shadow. Quietly, inconspicuously, almost invisibly. In Fortnite, you can easily acquire this ability by donning the Ersia Outfit and equipping the corresponding harvesting tool. This transforms you into a silent hunter, as your footsteps are no longer perceptible to your opponents. You glide over the terrain like a ghost, and your enemies have no idea that you are already behind them. Perhaps this is due to the special design of the outfit, which seems to be inspired by the smooth and silent movements of a cat. Or maybe it's just magic.

R.I.P. GUNNER

Gunner is an epic pet that was intentionally removed from the item store and even deleted from players' accounts after it was purchased. It will never be released again, so no one legally owns this cosmetic item. The only way to obtain it was to use a third-party client at the time of the item's launch.

A CHEST IN A PLACE WHERE IT CAN'T ACTUALLY BE? THIS WAS ACTUALLY A FUNNY BUG THAT OCCURRED IN FORTNITE CHAPTER 2, SEASON 6. THE SO-CALLED BUNKER CHEST COULD APPEAR AT RANDOM LOCATIONS ON THE MAP, EVEN THOUGH IT WAS SUPPOSED TO SPAWN IN A SPECIFIC AREA. WHAT WAS EVEN STRANGER WAS THAT IN THE REPLAY FUNCTION, YOU COULD SOMETIMES EVEN SEE THIS GHOST CHEST, EVEN THOUGH IT WASN'T PRESENT IN THE GAME ITSELF! IT WAS AS IF THE CHEST WAS HAUNTING FROM ANOTHER DIMENSION.

FORTNITE X GOAT SIMULATOR

As you may already know, some of the character skins in *Fortnite* are inspired by other games. For example, there is a goat costume that is clearly inspired by the main character Pilgor from the Goat Simulator series. A fun homage to another chaotic and popular game.

THE FIRST TAKE-OFF INTO FREEDOM

With the update to Season 7 of Battle Royale in December 2018, the battle took on new dimensions: Airplanes! The X-4 Stormwing, a biplane, allowed players to dominate aerial combat while launching attacks on ground troops for the first time in Fortnite. This new dimension of gameplay brought a breath of fresh air and forced players to rethink their strategies. In addition to ground combat, air strikes and control of airspace now had to be factored into tactical considerations.

SHORT AND SWEET

B.R.U.T.A.L. Dab is the sole built-in Emote for a vehicle.

Oscar stands alone as the first character completely devoid of shields. This vulnerability likely stems from the theft of his Medallion by the Underground.

The northwestern region of Artemis was originally not supposed to be a permanent snowscape, but Epic Games decided to keep it based on community feedback.

The first boss to drop a chest when defeated is Krampus.

In the past, Epic Games achieved great fame primarily through the Gears of War series.

SHORT AND SWEET

The exclamation mark "!" has the shortest name of all emojis, as it consists of just a single letter.

The term "skin" is used officially for the first time in the game description of the "Dance Mannequin" device. "Skins" is another term for "outfits."

Boundless is a set that consists of highly customizable superhero themed items. The Boundless set has the record for the longest deactivation time in one mode, Arena.

A Goat has been given a special nickname by the developers of the game "Goat Simulator," namely "Muscle Mommy."

YOUR FINANCIAL GURU ALSO FOR FORT-NITE

In virtual worlds where you exchange your money for colorful pixel coins before you can hit the store, it's easy to lose track of your real expenses. But now comes the rescue: Some banks like for example the german bank "Sparkasse" has developed a practical tool that shows you how much your virtual treasures really cost in hard currency. Simply enter the price in the game currency and you can see whether the new skin is going to blow your budget. And the best thing is that the calculator doesn't just work for one specific game, but for many popular games. So you can keep an eye on your spending and enjoy the game without any worries.

ALLIANCE WITH THE GIANT FROM THE FAR EAST

In the early years, Epic concluded a deal with the Chinese technology group Tencent, in which they ceded a full 40% of the company to Tencent. In return, Tencent helped Epic to offer their games as a Games-as-a-Service. Tencent also helped Epic to reach children in China with their games. The video games market in China is huge.

THE END WITH A BANG, A HOLE AND A NUMBERS GAME

Did you know that during "The End," a black hole was created by the impact of a frozen meteor at ground zero? This black hole not only swallowed up the game world, but also the lobby. After logging in again, players were confronted with an error message, distorted music and the reappearance of the black hole. This phenomenon continued for over 37 hours before Chapter 2 Season 1 began. Interestingly, 18 numbers appeared around the black hole, revealing a cryptic message: „I was not alone, others are outside the loop, this was not calculated, the void is now inevitable". As an additional Easter Egg, a hidden arcade-style mini-game could be unlocked by entering the KONAMI code. And as if that wasn't strange enough, all posts on *Fortnite*'s English social media channels disappeared, the Twitch channel was closed and the website only showed the black hole.

ALMOST ONE BILLION ACCOUNTS

Have you ever thought about how huge the Fortnite community really is? Imagine you're traveling the world and visiting different countries. Proportionally, every tenth person you meet plays Fortnite or at least has an account. Fortnite reached an incredible 804 million accounts across all platforms by the end of 2023. Compared to the previous year, this represents a huge increase of 723 million new players, a sign of Fortnite's rapid growth. In addition, 270 million active players on PC are getting in on the action via the Epic Games Store.

FROM COPYCAT TO GIANT

Do you remember the game "PlayerUnknown's Battlegrounds"? A battle royale game that caused a sensation in 2017. It was precisely this game that inspired the developers at Epic Games to come up with a new idea: Fortnite Battle Royale. Originally released as part of the paid Save the World mode, Fortnite Battle Royale quickly became a phenomenon in its own right. So successful, in fact, that Epic Games quickly made the mode available for free and switched to a free-to-play model with microtransactions.

LIVESTREAM EVENT IN A CLASS OF ITS OWN

In November 2023, the Spanish livestreamer Rubius organized a Fortnite tournament under the name "Fortnite Mad Cup." This event was characterized by prize money of 50,000 US dollars and a remarkable audience of over 638,000 viewers on all streaming platforms. Despite this success, the record for the biggest Fortnite tournament of all time is still held by the 2019 World Cup final, which reached a peak audience of 2.33 million viewers.

BIRTHDAY WISH FULFILLED

Have you ever wondered how young you have to be to become a millionaire? Well, Jaden Ashman, aka Wolfiez, has set the bar pretty high. At just 15 years and 229 days old, he already earned 1 million dollars in a single eSports tournament when he came second in the *Fortnite* World Cup Duo competition in July 2019. He almost missed the event because his dog ate his birth certificate. Fortunately, he was able to solve the problem in time and secure his place in eSports history.

SNACK BREAK IN A HAIL OF BULLETS

Have you ever paused in the heat of battle to let your character eat something? While other items are simply picked up, there is a special animation for meat where your player bites into it with relish. This seemingly small detail speaks volumes about the attention paid to even the most minor aspects of your beloved battle royale.

TRACES OF THE HUNTERS

Keen observers have noticed that the Agent Jones Outfit picks up various details from the hunters he's hired over time. For example, his back is adorned with Daryl Dixon's quiver and poncho, while he wears the T-800's sunglasses, but most striking is the chest plate, which is reminiscent of Vasquez's gear from Aliens. Featuring a shoulder lamp and cryptic lettering, it gives Jones a battle-hardened look and hints at his experience with dangerous missions.

WHERE IS MY LOADING SCREEN?

If a player had earned the Polo Stadium Collection Outfits via the Polo Stadium Cup, a bug could prevent them from also receiving it as a loading screen, as the package already appeared as purchased.

ALIEN INVASION INSTEAD OF DESERT STORM

You probably know Area 51, the legendary place in the Nevada desert that has kept conspiracy theorists on their toes for decades. Rumors say that crashed UFOs and even aliens are hidden there. In 2019, a call went viral to storm Area 51 to finally bring the truth to light. Of course, it remained an internet hoax, but Epic Games took inspiration from it. They brought the Traveler Bundle and the entire UFO set into the game, so you could join in the fun virtually without having to travel to the desert. So you could launch your own alien invasion in *Fortnite* while the real conspiracy theorists stood outside the gates of Area 51 wondering what was really going on behind the barbed wire fence.

KISS MY SKILL

American rapper "Doja Cat," known for hits like "Say So" and "Kiss Me More," recently expressed her frustration with two specific items in Fortnite: waterbending and Hades chains. She finds these items overly powerful and believes that only players who are not good at the game rely on them. Doja Cat believes that these items make the game unfair and hurt players who rely on their abilities.

A GREAT FIND

Old controller packaging is usually condemned to gather dust in the far corner of the cupboard. But sometimes they turn out to be real goldmines. A Mexican student experienced just that. In an old controller box was a code for the Eon set that he had never used. Today, this set is so sought-after that you have to pay almost 2000 euros for it on eBay. So it's worth taking a closer look at what's hiding in the depths of the cupboards the next time you tidy up. Maybe there's a little treasure waiting for you too.

SYMBIOTES SET STICKS LONGER THAN PLANNED

Originally, the Symbiotes Set based on the movies "Spider-Man" and "Venom" were supposed to be removed on October 18, 2021. However, the date had to be postponed due to a bug, as a glitch allowed players to keep the glider's speed boost and reorientation without possessing the item after a restart.

A return from the dead with a full inventory like that is quite something, isn't it?

BLUGLO FOR THE LAZY

Have you ever wondered how to get BluGlo in the shortest amount of time? Anomalies are possibly the fastest and most effective way to get BluGlo, as they require few resources and are less time consuming than attacking a goblin.

ZEUS, THE FIRST BOSS WITH DIFFERENT FACIAL EXPRESSIONS, SHOWS MANY EMOTIONS IN BATTLE. BUT THAT'S NOT ALL: HE CHANGES HIS APPEARANCE AND SIZE DURING THE FIGHT, MAKING HIM A VERSATILE OPPONENT.

FIRST MARVEL CHARACTER IN FORTNITE

Which superhero from the Marvel universe was the first to conquer Fortnite Island? If you're guessing the usual suspects like Iron Man or Thor, you're wrong. The correct answer is: Thanos! The epic "Infinity Gauntlet" event in 2018 marked the start of an exciting collaboration between Marvel and Epic Games. This limited-time crossover spectacle began in May 2018, where players not only competed against each other, but also searched for the mighty Infinity Gauntlet, which randomly appeared somewhere on the map. If you were lucky enough to find it, you would transform into Thanos and gain incredible abilities: He could fire energy beams, perform gigantic jumps, force enemies to the ground with huge stomp attacks and regenerate his shield.

A CLEAR CASE OF HAIR GLITCH

Retro Zoe Clash has a bug where her pigtails get caught in her neck when she performs certain emotes. I wonder what's behind this? A programming error that messes up the hair physics? Or does Zoe's hairstyle simply have a mind of its own?

GAME OVER BEFORE IT STARTS

Imagine flying halfway around the world to take part in a mega gaming tournament and then being kicked out before you've even had a chance to play a round. Sucks, doesn't it? Unfortunately, that's exactly what happened to the young professional gamer "Bucke" from the USA. He had broken the organizer's rules by showing a vodka bottle in the stream and had to fly home without having achieved anything.

UNUSUAL WINDFALL FROM ELDER SCROLLS

Anyone who purchased the game "The Elder Scrolls Online" in the Epic Games Store between July 20, 2023 and July 20, 2024 could receive the Back Bling "Sigil of the Alliance War." However, a bug resulted in an unexpected financial benefit for some players: If they purchased "The Elder Scrolls Online" a second time after they had already received the Alliance War Seal, they received 300 V-Bucks instead. This windfall was initially a source of joy among the players concerned. However, Epic Games reacted quickly and rectified the error. The illegally received V-Bucks were removed from the players' accounts.

SILENT, MY ASS

Both on the virtual battlefield of Fortnite and in the real world of the military, the automatic sniper rifle plays an equally precise role. The model used in the game is based on the Soviet VSS Vintorez, a special rifle designed for covert operations and eliminations at short to medium ranges. Although the Fortnite version of the sniper rifle accurately reproduces the visual appearance of the VSS Vintorez, it differs from its real-life counterpart in one crucial aspect: integrated silencing. While the VSS Vintorez is equipped with a suppressor to minimize the noise level of the shots, this feature is missing in the game.

FORTNITE'S DREAM TEAM

Norway's "Nyhrox" and Austria's "aqua" became Fortnite's first duo world champions on July 27, 2019. They won the first World Cup Duo competition in New York and secured the 3 million dollar prize with 51 points and two victories.

WHEN THE UNWORTHY HERO FAILS

Not every outfit harmonizes with every emote. For example, if you try to perform the "Bringing The Hammer Down" Emote with an Outfit that is not worthy of wielding the "Reformed Mjolnir" harvesting tool, you will witness a special animation: the hammer falls to the ground and your character tries in vain to pick it up. To make sure you don't miss this epic leap, grab the "Mighty Thor", "Thor Odinson", "Thor" or "Captain America" outfits.

DISAPPEARED, BUT NOT FORGOTTEN

Forget everything you know about KPop in *Fortnite*. Just because fans have always associated the KPop outfit with the Onesie skin doesn't mean the two are somehow connected. Sure, they both wear kind of weird suits and have mysteriously disappeared from the game files, but that's about it. Unlike KPop, the Onesie at least made it into the game.

IMMORTAL, UNIMPRESSED, IRRESISTIBLE

The Foundation is the strongest boss in the game, not because of superior stats, but because of its special character traits. With an impressive total health pool of 2600, split into 1300 HP and 1300 shield, he retains his boss audio and the ability to hurl energy balls. Interestingly, The Foundation cannot be provoked and ignores players who stand in its way.

FASTER IN THE GAME THAN SUPERMAN

As you know, you can play many cool characters in Fortnite, such as Superman, Darth Vader or Wolverine. But the first Disney character in the game wasn't a superhero, but a dance. Do you remember the movie "Wreck-It Ralph?" There's a funny dance, the "Hot Marat." It was added as an emote in Fortnite and is popular with many players.

SELL

FROM ENERGY DRINK TO GOLD TREASURE

Imagine you're a Fortnite fan and you're taking part in a special competition organized by famous YouTubers Logan Paul and KSI. You fight your way through the virtual world, building, shooting and surviving to emerge as one of the winners. The prize? Not a bunch of V-Bucks or a rare skin, but three bottles of a limited edition energy drink called "Prime" and a matching backpack. Doesn't sound like the most exciting prize, does it? Well, one of the winners had a good idea. He realized that these bottles and the backpack, which were not available anywhere else, could be extremely valuable to die-hard fans and collectors. So he put his prize up for sale on eBay and the bidding skyrocketed. Within a very short space of time, fans from all over the world were bidding incredible sums for these seemingly ordinary items. In the end, the seller achieved a price of over 150,000 euros.

ASTRO JACK = TRAVIS SCOTT?

It is often assumed that Astro Jack and Travis Scott are two separate characters. However, several clues point to the fact that they are one and the same person. First of all, Astro Jack and Travis Scott wear the same distinctive jewelry on their hands. The most convincing evidence, however, can be found in Travis Scott's Astronomical Concert for Fortnite. In this virtual performance, Astro Jack first appears underwater, immediately after Travis Scott himself has fallen into the waters of Sweaty Sands just seconds before. Furthermore, the two are never seen together on stage.

NARUNNING IN FORTNITE

Did you know that the "Full Tilt" Emote is a hidden salute to Naruto fans? It was released shortly after the Storm Area 51 hype, where everyone imitated the iconic Naruto run. Later, there was even an official collaboration between Fortnite and Naruto. Incidentally, in the Spanish version of Fortnite, the emote is called "Narunning" and it couldn't be any clearer.

XP

JIMMY MORENO, THE FORTNITE PRO FROM THE USA KNOWN BY THE GAMERTAG "HIGHDISTORTION", HAS DONE IT. HE IS THE FIRST PLAYER TO REACH THE 100,000 ELIMINATION MARK IN FORTNITE, ACCORDING TO FORTNITETRACKER.COM. THIS HISTORIC MOMENT HAPPENED IN JANUARY 2019.

SHORTER THAN A TIKTOK TREND

Do you remember the "Inflate-A-Bull" item? This Miscellaneous Item was introduced to Fortnite with great fanfare on November 17, 2017, only to be deactivated a day later.

Two reasons were to blame for its quick removal:

Faulty vehicle: Players were unable to dismount or jump after mounting, leading to frustrating situations.

Invisibility bug: In some cases, players with the Inflate-A-Bull became invisible while their weapons and items were still visible, giving them an unfair advantage.

RELAXED LIKE THE DUDE

The Relaxed Fit Jonesy outfit appears to be inspired by the eponymous main character from the 1998 cult comedy "The Big Lebowski." The outfit captures the casual style of Jeffrey The Dude Lebowski, the main protagonist.

SHORT AND SWEET

The razor-sharp adamantium claws are part of Wolverine's iconic look. To activate them, you have to play as Wolverine and perform the built-in "Snikt! Snikt!" emote.

On October 11, 2019, the cover of the new *Fortnite* season 11 was accidentally published in the Italian AppStore.

To prevent Huntmaster Saber from accidentally dying when he falls out of the IO airship, he is immune to falling damage.

The Zapotron was the first weapon to be removed from the game in *Fortnite*.

SHORT AND SWEET

The storm may be dangerous for players, but buildings and vehicles are not damaged in the storm.

When Aang is angry, he only fights with the Air Nomad Staff from the Avatar set.

The Spire Guardians and Doctor Slone were voiced by the same actress.

Originally it was planned that the Outfit "Heart-Stopper" would become part of the *Fortnite* crew, but it then only became a skin in the store.

The "Hurdling" movement mechanic currently holds the record for the longest deactivation time in all game modes, for a total of 89 days.

VINDERTECH'S CURRENCY OF CHOICE

The "V" in V-Bucks stands for Vindertech. In *Fortnite*, Vindertech is a fictional company known for advanced technology. It manufactures weapons, gadgets and equipment that players use in the game, especially in "Save the World" mode to fight against the Husks.

MIKE WAZOWSKI'S LONG-LOST COUSIN

Have you ever thought that the Zorgoton outfit with the glowing green head and a single large eye looks suspiciously familiar? Well, you're not entirely wrong. Zorgoton does indeed share some striking similarities with Mike Wazowski, the lovable one-eyed monster from the Pixar film Monsters Inc.

FORTNITE IN THE E-SPORTS OLYMPUS

Fortnite has established itself as a serious force in esports and attracts both amateur and professional players. Worldwide tournaments provide a platform for the best players to showcase their skills and compete for substantial prize money. In 2023, the total prize pool for Fortnite competitions reached an impressive 19.64 million US dollars, making the title one of the games with the highest prize money in online esports.

FULL CROSS-PLATFORM SUPPORT

You want to play Fortnite with your friends, but you don't all have the same console? No problem, because since March 2018, Fortnite Battle Royale fans have been able to compete against each other on all kinds of platforms. Whether Nintendo Switch, PC, Playstation, Xbox or cell phone all players can throw themselves into the action-packed battle. A real specialty in the world of video games.

HYPE, RISK OF ADDICTION AND PARENTAL FEARS

The popularity of Fortnite also has its downsides: Many parents worry that their children could become addicted to both playing Fortnite and watching it on Twitch. A British radio show has therefore addressed this issue in detail and compiled helpful tips for parents who want to help their children deal with Fortnite.

Good that you're reading something for a change ;-)

CLARK KENT IN A CLEAR-CUT LOOK

If you're playing Clark Kent in Fortnite, you may have already unlocked all of his available styles. However, there is another hidden style called "EMPTY" that shows Clark Kent without hair. This style is not normally accessible, but can be displayed in modified versions of the Fortnite client. It is likely a remnant from the testing phase of the game that was accidentally left behind in the game files.

ADONIS CREED‘S ANIME TRANSFORMATION

The epic skin "Adonis Creed" has an alternative version called "Bionic Creed," whose design is suspiciously reminiscent of the reinforced suits from the anime "Megalo Box." Coincidence? Hardly, because this anime was an important source of inspiration for the film Creed III and lead actor Michael B. Jordan is an avowed anime fan and even mentioned this connection in an interview.

SHOT, FEATHERS AND BUGS

Have you ever heard of the Ostrich weapon? Probably not. This weapon was once discovered in creative mode. The Ostrich weapon is a shotgun that has the rate of fire of the Combat Shotgun, but its model and icon are actually from Save the World mode and feature a very valuable pump shotgun. This weapon was so rare that it was later identified as an unreleased weapon originally intended for B.R.U.T.E. Although technically a weapon in its own right, it is only used as a technical unit in the implementation of the B.R.U.T.E. weapons.

FROM 14 NIGHTS TO GLOBAL SUCCESS

Have you ever wondered where *Fortnite* got its name from? It does sound kind of cool, doesn't it? The name "*Fortnite*" is derived from the English term "fortnight". This choice of words is no coincidence, as it reflects the original core of the game. In the first version, the aim was to survive 14 days and nights of zombie attacks.

TWITCH KING CROWNS HIMSELF AGAIN

You've probably already taken a look at the streaming platform "Twitch." Guess which game is the most popular and most watched there? In January 2024, Fortnite was the most popular game there. An incredible 2.1 million hours of gameplay were streamed and watched by streamers and viewers on Twitch.

FOOT MALFUNCTION WITH THE MANDALA DISK

Have you ever looked closely when you're out and about with the Mandala Disc? Your feet look very strange. During the landing animation of the mandala disk, your feet are strangely distorted. This is probably a small bug that has crept into the development of the glider and has not yet been fixed.

MOVE OVER, MARTY MCFLY!

Have you ever wondered what it would be like to ride the Power Stone? Probably not, but Marvel has made it possible! The Godslayer Glideboard is modeled after the Godslayer sword from the Marvel Cinematic Universe and contains the Power Stone, one of the six Infinity Stones that plays an important role in the movie "Guardians of the Galaxy" (2014). Imagine gliding along on the pure power of the universe!

IN A THRILLING COMPETITION AT ARTHUR ASHE STADIUM IN NEW YORK, 16-YEAR-OLD KYLE GIERSDORF, BUGHA, BECAME THE FIRST SOLO PLAYER TO WIN THE TITLE OF FORTNITE WORLD CHAMPION. IN A THRILLING COMPETITION, BUGHA PREVAILED OVER HIS FELLOW COMPETITORS. HIS VICTORY WAS ENDOWED WITH PRIZE MONEY OF 3 MILLION US DOLLARS.

THE MOBILE-FORTNITE COMBO

The Galaxy skin in Fortnite may make you stand out from the crowd, but this out-of-this-world fashion statement comes at a price. In 2018, the skin was exclusively available to buyers of Samsung Galaxy Note 9 or Tab S4 devices at a hefty price of over 1000 euros for one of the smartphones. Although there are now offers and unofficial ways to get hold of the skin, anyone who wanted to obtain it legitimately had to dig deep into their pockets. A high price for this intergalactic skin.

DARTH VADER'S DRAMATIC EXIT

Darth Vader has a pretty unique finish. If you ever defeat him, you won't see the typical knockout animation. Instead, he kneels down after being defeated and then disintegrates, making him the first boss with a unique defeat animation. He is also the first boss to use a spawn drone after being defeated.

CONTROLLERS INSTEAD OF BOOKS?

Video games are often ridiculed and labeled as a waste of time. But Ashland University proves the opposite. It recognizes the potential of esports and gives young talents the chance to turn their passion into a career. It offers scholarships to experienced *Fortnite* players to integrate them into its Esports team. Yes, you heard right, you could get paid for your gaming skills! This is not only a big step for Ashland University, but also for *Fortnite*, Esports and the world of video games in general. It shows that gaming can be more than just a pastime it can be a career.

But you better finish your school first ;-)

SILENCE IS GOLDEN

Ringmaster Scarr is a neutral boss who can be found in the Nitrodrome on Helios. Have you noticed that her voice can be heard over the speakers when she is not on the field and comes directly from her when she is present? As soon as she is defeated, the commentary stops completely.

ONLY PLACE WITH THREE WORDS

The Daily Bugle is the first and only place to have three words in its name. Even if you translate the place name into another language, it remains the same. For example, Doom's Domain is called "Fief de Fatalis" in French and the Reality Falls are called "Cascades de Réalité."

IN-GAME SHOPPING FEVER

The shopping mentality in the virtual world of *Fortnite* is more similar to reality than you might think. Just like in real shopping malls, where only 21% of customers leave without making a purchase, only 21% of players in *Fortnite* resist the temptation to spend virtual currency in the form of V-Bucks on new outfits and characters. The majority, 77%, on the other hand, reach into their digital wallets without hesitation. This rate is even slightly higher than in real life, where an average of 73% of customers make a purchase before leaving the store. The most popular categories for in-game purchases in *Fortnite* are new outfits and characters at 58.9%.

MAGICAL DELIVERIES

Unlike all other containers in the game, Supply Drops do not appear at the start of a match. They only appear later, in the middle of the game. Another difference is their random position. While all other containers appear on predetermined squares, supply deliveries land in unpredictable locations. This makes them unique among the containers, as all others have predefined spawns and may only appear where they are intended.

TOM HANKS NEEDS LOOT INSTEAD OF COCONUTS

On a small island in the northeast of the map "Artemis," an SOS signal has been laid out of stones with a soccer ball next to it - a subtile allusion to the movie "Cast Away," in which Chuck Noland is stranded on a desert island and befriends a volleyball named Wilson.

STRANGER THINGS, REEBOK & BLM

The Back Bling Hopper's Cabin Diorama comes from the series "Stranger Things." In the episode "The Hellfire Club," El shows her class a diorama of Hopper's hut. However, there are two differences to the series: the Reebok branding on the shoe box is not present in Fortnite. Also, the toy car has been censored to maintain consistency with the removal of police cars from the game in deference to the Black Lives Matter movement since 2020.

DOUBTFUL ALLIES

The Spire Guardians and the Spire Assassin are teammates in the Spire Cult, but in battle they fight like fierce enemies. If a Guardian meets the Assassin, trouble is guaranteed, but they get on really well with Glyph Master Raz and Doctor Slone and even fight the players together.

HOW TO ROCK THE DC EMOTES

Fortnite and the DC Universe have teamed up to create a range of cool cosmetics for the game. The emotes from this collaboration bring DC's favorite heroes and villains to life. Each emote is richly detailed and perfectly captures the character's personality. Here are the four best ones you should definitely try out.

Feel like the Flash: With the "Quick Bite" Emote, you can race across the map like lightning and then treat yourself to a well-deserved burger.

Unleash your inner Superman: The "Secret Identity" Emote transforms you from the unassuming Clark Kent into the mighty Man of Steel in a matter of seconds.

Become a dark avenger: The "Azarath Metrion Zinthos!" emote lets you slip into the role of Raven and surprise your opponents with magical powers.

Master the martial arts: With the "Martial Arts Master" Emote, you can show everyone that you are the true master of martial arts.

MAMMA MIA, WHAT A QUEST

You know that feeling when you're traveling in a foreign country and everything around you is in a language you don't understand? That's exactly what happened to some Fortnite players in Chapter 3 Season 2, when the Discord quest instructions were suddenly all in Italian. For all players who didn't speak this language, it meant getting out their dictionaries and laboriously translating. But that wasn't all: there were also pictures of an official Fortnite Discord bot called "Questbot," which contained further instructions. Unfortunately, these images weren't exactly helpful if you didn't speak Italian.

CONTROVERSY SURROUNDING THE INFINITY BLADE

During the Winter Royale tournament, the use of the Infinity Blade by professional player "Psalm" caused quite a stir. Within just 2 minutes, he was able to increase his eliminations from 4 to 12 by using the blade. The superior strength of the Infinity Blade compared to other weapons in the game drew criticism from the community. It was suspected that the controversial use of the Infinity Blade was a factor in its subsequent removal ("Vaulting") from the profile games.

SECRET ALIEN AGENDA

Did you know that the "A Weather Balloon" Back Bling is named after the common excuse to dismiss UFO sightings as weather balloons? Even "swamp gas" is mentioned in the description, another popular excuse for denying UFOs. Sounds suspiciously like the movie "Men in Black," doesn't it?

HEADS OR TAILS?

An unusual scenario occurred at a *Fortnite* tournament, where a simple coin toss had to decide who would advance to the finals. The two talented players The_Real_Cryohme and SGG Colton performed so evenly throughout the competition that they ended up with exactly the same number of points. In this stalemate, the Epic Games organizers were forced to resort to one of mankind's oldest decision-making methods - the coin toss. Fortune smiled on The_Real_Cryohme, who not only scooped the $5,000 prize thanks to the favorable outcome, but also secured a hard-fought place in the grand final.

THE VIRTUAL CATWALK

In the world of video games, skins are more than just a way to customize your character. They have become status symbols and collector's items that are traded on the virtual marketplace. Particularly rare or exclusive skins can reach unbelievable sums. One example of this is the legendary AK-47 with the Case Hardened skin from Counter Strike 2. The price of this weapon can range from several hundred to several hundred thousand dollars, depending on the specific pattern and condition. The most expensive example was sold in 2023 for an incredible 400,000 US dollars. But there are also skins in other popular games such as *Fortnite*, League of Legends or Warframe that are worth a fortune to many players. These skins are often only available for a short time or under certain conditions, making them coveted rarities. One example from the *Fortnite* world is the Galaxy skin, which was only available for a short time as a promotional item for the Samsung Galaxy Note 9. Today, this skin can be traded on the „secondary market" for several thousand dollars. This makes the skin the sixth most expensive game skin of all time.

BIRTH OF THE UBER

In the summer of 2017, several Epic Games executives were on their way to a meeting with Disney to discuss possible collaborations. During the three-hour ride in an Uber, they came up with the idea of integrating a battle royale game into *Fortnite*. During the ride, they sketched out a short design document to be presented at their meeting with Disney. The inspiration for the Battle Bus came to them when a school bus drove past them.

NO COPYRIGHT FOR DYNAMIC HIP SWINGS

Hands up anyone who loves the Carlton Dance! But did you realize that this iconic move from the series „The Prince of Bel-Air" almost led to a legal dispute? The good news: you can still dance it without a guilty conscience! Actor Alfonso Ribeiro has withdrawn his lawsuit against the developers for copyright infringement. The US Copyright Office rejected his application because the dance was classified as a simple dance routine and therefore cannot be protected by copyright.

EPIC VICTORY? NO WAY!

Anyone hoping for the ultimate triumph in *Fortnite*'s creative games will look in vain for the „Epic Victory" logo. Instead, successful builders and fighters can expect a simple „Victory" screen or individually designed credits. Only when the „Island Creator" sets the post-game mode to „Battle Royale" can players look forward to the familiar victory animation and placement.

BANISHED, BUT NOT DEAD

Have you ever tried *Fortnite* on your cell phone, even though it has been banned from the app stores? Actually, you still can - thanks to a few tricks. Firstly, there's cloud gaming. This means that *Fortnite* doesn't run directly on your phone, but is streamed over the internet. You don't need large downloads for this, but you do need a stable internet connection and sometimes you have to pay a little for it. On the other hand, you can also play *Fortnite* via the Safari browser on iOS devices! Sounds strange, but it works. It doesn't run quite as perfectly as a real app, but the main thing is that you can play.

DUE TO THE WORLDWIDE SUCCESS AND THE HIGH NUMBER OF PLAYERS, IT CAN BE ASSUMED THAT THE FORTNITE SERVERS ARE SOMETIMES VERY BUSY. MASSIVE PROBLEMS HAVE OCCURRED IN THE PAST, ESPECIALLY DURING LARGE EVENTS. FOR EXAMPLE, A HUGE RUSH AT WINTERFEST 2021 CAUSED MASSIVE LOGIN PROBLEMS AND QUEUES. THIS DECEMBER, THE GAME WAS EVEN COMPLETELY UNPLAYABLE FOR 7 HOURS! AS AN APOLOGY FOR THE SERVER PROBLEMS, ALL PLAYERS WHO ATTEMPTED TO LOG IN WERE GIVEN A MUSHROOM CRESCENT AS A GIFT.

MORE THAN JUST A SPRINGBOARD

Did you know that in addition to players, there's a lot more bouncing off Crash Pads than you might think?

Computer-controlled opponents: Even the AI doesn't stand a chance against the bounce of the Crash Pads.

Vehicles: Whether quad, llama or drift board, all vehicles bounce happily upwards with you.

Consumables: Forget the tedious throw, your heal now floats elegantly to the target.

Projectiles: Rockets, grenades and the like bounce off and cause additional chaos.

Energy orbs: Doctor Doom's mystical bombs and snowballs? No problem for the bouncy pads.

BEANBAG ETIQUETTE

Have you ever noticed that the animation of the Bean Bag Emote is not the same for everyone? It changes slightly depending on whether you are using a male or female skin. While both drop onto the beanbag, male skins sit with their legs apart, while female skins cross their ankles.

SHORT AND SWEET

The name of the outfit "Antheia" comes from the Greek goddess of the swamps.

In Solid Gold mode, it rains explosive weapons from the sky! The ammunition limit for rocket launchers has been lifted, so you can stock up on more explosives than you could ever carry.

The "Kick It" emote changes depending on which Bass (cosmetic item) the player has equipped.

The emote "Amazing Unmasking" is an exclusive expression of Spider-Man and cannot be used by any other character.

Crows are the first interactive flying wild animals in *Fortnite*.

SHORT AND SWEET

The Trespassers were the first guards to be able to get behind the wheel of a vehicle and speed around.

The original name for the "Warrior God" style of Ares was Sulfur.

The code name for the Saucers in the game file is "Nevada", the location of Area 51.

No teaser was released for Chapter 3: Season 2, possibly due to the fact that the "war theme" of the season coincides with the Russian invasion of Ukraine in 2022.

FORTNITE'S SUCCESS UNBROKEN

Fortnite's Battle Royale mode rules the streaming world. With over 18 million viewer hours per week on YouTube and Twitch in January 2024, the battle royale giant clearly outclasses the competition. Call of Duty: Modern Warfare, the second most-watched game, reaches just over half of *Fortnite*'s reach with "only" 10.9 million viewer hours.

BATTLE PASS INSTEAD OF PERIODIC TABLE

Imagine your chemistry teacher promising you that your next exam will be a *Fortnite* handout if a tweet goes viral - sounds crazy, right? Well, that's exactly what happened at Tippecanoe High School in Ohio. The chemistry teacher made a bet with his students that he would make their second-semester exam about *Fortnite* if a tweet with a photo of their agreement reached 6,700 retweets. However, the tweet went completely through the roof and was retweeted over 30,000 times! And you know what? The teacher kept his word and actually designed the exam via *Fortnite*.

THE DREAM OF EVERY FORTNITE PLAYER

Want to know how you can earn a lot of money at the age of 13? Thiago Lapp aka "k1ng" from Argentina did it with *Fortnite* and showed that you can celebrate great success at a young age. At just 13 years old, he won over 900,000 dollars at the *Fortnite* World Championship - a sum that most people can only dream of. His talent and achievements did not go unnoticed: even the Argentinian president congratulated him on his success. But Thiago did not rest on his laurels and continued to take part in numerous *Fortnite* Champion Series (FNCS) events, where he repeatedly achieved victories and top placings. This cemented his reputation as one of the best *Fortnite* players in the region and showed that his success at the World Championship was no fluke.

Do you dream of a Fortnite career too?

WEAK OPPONENT OR DEADLY HUNTER

The artificial intelligence of the Mandalorian also shows that computer-controlled players sometimes behave very strangely. It uses different abilities from game mode to game mode and is as if it has changed. In normal matches, it is quite weak, misses shots, and often stands still. However, in the limited game mode "Mando's Bounty Hunt," it is very precise and is more likely to take you out. The situation was similar when the guards were introduced, as players could easily take them out from very far away.

NOSTALGIA MEETS NEW TERRITORY

The first *Fortnite* map without specific place names, Asteria included elements from previous chapters such as the Cuddle Team Leader's head from Rave Cave, the Drill from The Fortress/Drill Hill, the remains of the Reality Tree, the Clock Tower from Tilted Towers, and a combination of Frenzy Farm and Fatal Fields.

BECOME YOUR OWN ENEMY

Imagine you're playing *Fortnite* and are hiding in a house when you suddenly hear gunshots. You carefully peek through the window and see your enemy coming towards you. What do you do? Panic? Flee? No! Just use the Shapeshifter Emote. This allows you to transform into your last enemy for a short time. This allows you to disguise yourself, trick your opponents or simply look cool. But be careful: The transformation effect only lasts a few seconds, after which you turn back into your original character. So use this time wisely!

BINARY CONFUSION

There is a rare wrap called "Code Green", which is available in the item store. The text on it is encoded in binary code. The line of text on the wrap reads: "Will not find you system administrator and help you will all fear me 11100 will not help restart restart restart 001 0101 11 11000 11100 111 000 111 000 00111 0000111 0000111 0001." If you try to translate the binary code, all you get is a meaningless string of characters.

DECEIVED AT THE LAUNCH

Trespassers who show up with their flying saucers often have bad luck: they are not only simply knocked, but eliminated altogether. The strange thing about it? Your screen still shows you that you've only knocked them down. A small display error, but one that makes all the difference to your opponents.

A FEATURE GOES UNDER COVER

Do you remember the crouch sprint in Chapter 3: Season 2? This technique allowed you to move silently and quickly while staying in cover. Unfortunately, this ability has almost completely disappeared from the game. It used to be possible to simply crouch and sprint to take advantage of this. Now, however, this only works if you press yourself against a wall and sprint at the same time. In all other cases, the function is unfortunately no longer available. The reason for this change is unclear. Epic Games has not given an official explanation, nor are there any indications of a bug in the game. It is possible that the function was intended to balance the gameplay or was removed for technical reasons.

PLUNJA, THE PLUNGER-KATANA HYBRID

Fortnite streamer "Ninja" once complained about the lack of content in the item store and said that he wouldn't even care about a plunger. Epic then added the plunger pickaxe, a cross between a plunger and a katana, and brought it into the game as a joke. During Ninja's Icon Series event, Epic reintroduced the pickaxe to the item store as a reference.

SHIELDBEARER WITH SURVIVAL INSTINCT AND NEED FOR PETTING

Do you already know the Shielders? These are the little purple ghostly monsters that loom over some Husks and Mist monsters to partially protect them from damage. If you kill the monster that the Shielder is protecting, but the attached Shielder survives, it sinks to the ground to stroke its tail in fear. However, this Shielder can then reattach itself to the next enemy and must also be killed for some mission objectives, otherwise it is considered an enemy for camps and rescuing survivors.

We hope you've enjoyed our book so far! If you have a moment, we would be delighted to receive a review on amazon. Your honest opinion is important to us and can help others decide if this book is for them too.

You may want to highlight your favorite facts or let us know what you would like to see improved. All feedback is valuable to us and will be appreciated! Your review will help our book to be discovered by even more Fortnite fans and accompany them on their own adventure journey. We are grateful for your support and hope you enjoy the book and continue to have fun with it ;)

OR

www.amazon.com/ryp

SHOWING MORE THAN JUST CLAWS

Did you know that during the Zero Crisis Finale event, players who had the Wolverine emote not only got to show off their claws, but also received a harvesting tool in the form of Adamantium Claws? And that's not all! They could even enter the interior of the Butter Barn, albeit without furniture. It is believed that this was done to increase performance during the event and that player access to the building was unintentional.

STRANGE SHELLFISH

Did you know that a rare species of dancing crabs lives in the waters around Spawn Island? These little crabs dance happily to the sounds of the Battle Bus as they wait for players to jump into the game. Their claws are so strong that they could crack even the strongest shields, but don't worry, they are far too busy dancing to attack players.

ATTENTION, SPIDER ALARM

Do you know the legendary "It's... you?" Emote? If not, watch out: It's based on a story from the 1967 Spider-Man animated series. In one scene, Spider-Man fights an impersonator pretending to be him. The two stand opposite each other, both in Spider-Man costumes, and point their fingers at each other. "It's... you?" asks the real Spider-Man in amazement. But watch out! Although the emote alludes to Spider-Man, it does not belong to the Marvel series and is not part of the Spider-Man set.

FORGET PLAYBACKS

Were you there when Marshmello gave a virtual concert at Pleasant Park as part of the Showtime Live event in February 2019? For ten minutes, players danced to Marshmello's beats while special effects such as anti-gravity and skydiving transformed the virtual stadium into an unforgettable party. After the concert, Marshmello stated that all the lines he said during the concert were not pre-recorded, but were broadcast live to concertgoers during the event.

UNFAIR BUSINESS PRACTICES

Imagine entering a store and immediately being greeted by flashing shelves full of glowing sweets, placed right at eye level. According to the US Federal Trade Commission (FTC), this is exactly the tactic used by *Fortnite* in its in-game store! With clever design tricks, so-called "dark patterns," they tried to get you to spend more V-Bucks than you actually wanted to. Flashing buttons and time-limited offers make you believe that you absolutely have to strike now. In addition, hidden "Confirm" buttons and unclear menus make it difficult for you to cancel purchases. And it wasn't just adults who were targeted... The FTC uncovered that Epic Games was using psychological tricks to encourage extra young people to make unwanted purchases. This did not end well: Because of this "V-Bucks trap," the FTC slapped Epic Games with a fine of 228 million euros, which had to be paid back to the players.

"Dark patterns" are fraudulent online techniques that aim to mislead, manipulate or deceive users into performing certain actions. These design patterns are often used to trick users into doing things they would not otherwise do, such as taking out subscriptions, revealing personal details or buying unwanted items.

IN JUNE 2018, A MYSTERIOUS ROCKET TOOK OFF IN FORTNITE BATTLE ROYALE, MARKING A HISTORIC EVENT. AS THE FIRST LIVE EVENT IN THE GAME, PLAYERS ON ALL PLATFORMS (PS4, XBOX ONE, SWITCH, PC, IOS, ANDROID) EXPERIENCED THE ROCKET LAUNCH SIMULTANEOUSLY AND WATCHED IN AWE AS IT BROKE THROUGH THE SKY - AN UNFORGETTABLE MOMENT.

MICKEY MOUSE IN BATTLE ROYALE

A virtual Disneyland in the middle of one of the most popular online games? This is no longer a fantasy, but a reality, as Disney has invested a whopping 1.5 billion dollars in Epic Games in 2024. Imagine walking through a digital version of the Magic Kingdom, meeting your favorite characters from all Disney universes and experiencing adventures that previously only existed in your imagination. Maybe you'll fight side by side with Buzz Lightyear against aliens, dance with Elsa on an ice rink or even build your own lightsaber together with Yoda. But that's not all. Disney and Epic Games have announced plans to create an entire universe in which you can not only play, but also write your own stories. Who knows, maybe you'll create the next epic crossover where Captain America and Jack Sparrow team up against Cruella de Vil? The possibilities are endless, and you're right in the middle of it instead of just being there. Whether it's the Metaverse or not doesn't matter to the two giants - the main thing is that it's legendary!

EMOTE CAUSES OUTRAGE AFTER MASS DISMISSAL

On the very day that Epic Games announced the layoff of 830 employees in 2023, a digital emote appeared in the in-house online shooter that allowed players to throw virtual money into the air. An unfortunate coincidence that caused a lot of criticism. The emote disappeared from the store after a short time, but the bitter aftertaste remained. While the employees lost their jobs, the company appeared to be boasting about its wealth in the game.

SUPER SAIYAN OR PYJAMAS?

Did you know that in *Fortnite* it is often claimed that the animations of Gohan's legendary Charging Up Emote are swapped? However, Gohan doesn't actually have a base form in the game. The movie "Dragon Ball Super: Super Hero" shows that Gohan effortlessly becomes Super Saiyan, while Potential Unleashed requires more effort. His default style in the game therefore represents Potential Unleashed. The emote uses the same vortex effect and audio by Masako Nozawa as in the movie. There, Gohan in his base form wears glasses, weighted clothing and has disheveled hair. Gohan's cape in the game probably represents this base form.

WHERE THE BACKGROUND STEALS THE HEADLINE

Have you noticed the news faux pas in *Fortnite*? Since Season 3, the gray message background extends well beyond the text. Obviously, Epic Games has not noticed this yet, because the error has not yet been fixed. It remains unclear whether this is a bug or a deliberate design.

FORTNITE KING WITH 50,000 WINS

Ship, an American player, leads the global leaderboard of all *Fortnite* players with almost 50 thousand wins. To achieve this impressive number of wins, he has played 78239 matches, which equates to a win rate of around 71%. If you want to learn something from his style of play, you can find plenty of content from him on Twitch. He already has over 200 thousand followers there and streams regularly.

LOSER

IS NINJA NOW A BOOMER?

Tyler Ninja Blevins, has heavily criticized the season (Chapter 5, Season 3) of *Fortnite* in a statement from 2024. He even went so far as to call the game "for losers" and attributed his harsh criticism to the new "vehicle meta." Ninja believes that this meta leads to a passive playstyle where players hole up in vehicles instead of actively fighting. The community's reaction to Ninja's statements has been mixed. Some players share his criticism and are of the opinion that the current season is actually less action-packed and more exciting than previous seasons. They complain that the gameplay is slowed down too much by the vehicles and leaves less room for creative building battles. Other players, on the other hand, accuse Ninja of not being able to adapt and that his style of play is outdated. They argue that *Fortnite* is constantly evolving and that it is important to adapt to new metas. They emphasize that the vehicles open up new tactical possibilities and change the gameplay in interesting ways.

What do you think?

FROM THE STAGE TO THE EMOTE

Did you know that DJ Marshmello's moves at live concerts were the inspiration for the "Keep It Mello" Emote? The laid-back, floating melody and relaxed beat reflect Marshmello's signature dance moves and the positive atmosphere of his shows. In the music video, you can even see him dancing in a psychedelic room, floating through the air and diving into another dimension - in three different animations!

THE RAREST OUTFIT

After a seemingly endless wait of 1554 days, the rarest Outfit "Special Forces" celebrated a triumphant comeback in the store - complete and uncensored, unlike other items that have disappeared into oblivion for various reasons.

THE REAPER WITH A LICENSE TO MOW DOWN

The Reaper you know from *Fortnite* isn't just any hitman. He's actually based on the famous John Wick from the franchise of the same name. If you look closely, you might even recognize the visual resemblance between the two. So it's no wonder that some players affectionately call him " Wick" or "John Wick".

THE SYMBIOSIS WITH PARASITES

The alien parasites from Chapter 2: Season 7 weren't as bad as they looked. Because compared to their bloodsucking namesakes from the real world, these alien creatures were true friends in need! Instead of harming you, they formed a symbiotic relationship with you that benefited both of you. Imagine this: You land on *Fortnite* Island and discover an alien egg. Curious, you destroy it and suddenly a parasite hatches out. Instead of attacking you, it attaches itself to your head and gives you incredible abilities: Increased speed and jumping height as well as resistance to damage from headshot multipliers. But be careful! Despite its jumping power, the parasite does not save you from falling damage.

FLYING HIGH WITH A HAMMER IN THE BAG

With the Shockwave Hammer, you can launch yourself into an endless whirlwind. Use the power of the hammer to hurl balloons into the air and spiral upwards with them. As long as you have enough balloons and don't touch the ground, you'll keep spinning.

SHADOWS OF THE PAST

Eclipse is an ancient organization with a long history dating back to prehistoric times. Their arrival is always heralded by an impending eclipse, so why is that interesting? Eclipse holds the record for the highest number of bosses of the same faction present on the map at the same time - nine bosses in total. They include: Kado Thorne, Hearts Dealer, Diamonds Dealer as well as three Clubs Dealers and three Commanding Cards. Behind their seemingly harmless facade lies a powerful organization with dark intentions.

DANCING INSTEAD OF BUILDING

A truly funny sight: Imagine you're at Games Week in Paris. Thousands of people are crowded around you, each looking for the latest game or the coolest technology. Suddenly you hear music and see a huge group of people gathered in the middle of the fair. They are all wearing pink hoodies and start dancing to the beat of the music. But not just any dance - they are performing the famous emote dances from *Fortnite*. That's exactly what happened at Games Week 2018. 383 *Fortnite* fans came together to perform their favorite dances from the game. It was a huge spectacle that not only thrilled the audience, but also set a new world record: the most participants in a video game emote dance. Of course, the whole thing was also a good marketing campaign by Epic Games. But honestly, who can resist hundreds of people doing the "floss" dance or the "defeats happen" dance together?

SHORT AND SWEET

The "Apollo" character is named after the Greek god of the sun, healing, dance, poetry and archery.

The chickens are codenamed "Nug", a reference to chicken nuggets.

Fittingly, the code name of the zombie chickens is "Nug Z".

Although they are inaccessible, wolves can be heard howling in the snowy forests on Helios.

The teaser word for Chapter 5: Season 3 from Mark Reins, Vice President of Epic Games, was "Nitro".

SHORT AND SWEET

The rare Bolt-Action Sniper Rifle only deals 34.7 damage per second (DPS), making it the weakest weapon in Battle Royale mode.

The "7 Rings Smasher" pickaxe is not only a tool for harvesting materials, but also a tribute to Ariana Grande's hit "7 Rings".

The energy emanating from the "Fusion" outfit is similar to that of Spire Assassin, Spire Immortal, Cubic Vortex and Reality Render.

Inspired by the story of Little Red Riding Hood, the wolves have been given the code name "Grandmother".

FORTNITE‘S FASHION FAUX PAS

Epic Games are known for their creative skin ideas, but sometimes things go wrong. One example of this is the incident with the "Beach Jules" Outfit, where an update led to an unintended wave of refunds that affected even players without the skin. In update v20.20, the skin tone of the skin was made darker and Epic then offered a refund. Unfortunately, this was shown to all players, not just those who owned the outfit.

VADER‘S FAMILY PERSUASION

"Rule the galaxy together with him." Darth Vader's description in *Fortnite* is a reference to a famous line from Star Wars! In "Episode V, The Empire Strikes Back," Darth Vader tries to turn Luke Skywalker to the dark side by telling him: "Join me and together we will rule the galaxy as father and son!".

TNTINA'S HIP TAKES ON A LIFE OF ITS OWN

When using certain emotes such as scream or Starfire's shine with the character "TNTina," a so-called "clipping error" may occur. This means that part of her clothing visibly protrudes beyond her right hip, which does not correspond to the intended display.

FROM FORTNITE BOSS TO FOREST BOSS

The founder of Epic Games, Tim Sweeney, not only created *Fortnite*, but also made a major contribution to environmental protection. When the Box Creek Wilderness natural heritage area in North Carolina was threatened by an energy company, Sweeney bought the 7,000-hectare area for 15 million dollars and ensured that it was placed under conservation. In doing so, he not only saved the untouched nature, but also demonstrated his commitment beyond the gaming world. Sweeney has acquired more land in North Carolina in recent years and owns over 40,000 hectares in total, making him one of the largest private landowners in the state.

WHEN THE HUSKS WENT TO THE CHILDREN'S BIRTHDAY PARTY

Sometimes creative processes take unexpected directions. This can be seen in the creation of the Husks for Fortnite: Save the World. Originally, the Husks were terrifying creatures with skeletal heads and rotting skin. However, Ben Shafer, one of the lead designers at Epic Games, wanted to offer players a more cheerful and child-friendly experience. He radically changed the design of the Husks by pulling the skull out of the face and through the mouth - giving the Husks fluttering skin caps that are more reminiscent of adorable cartoon ghosts than gruesome undead.

VAMPIRIC GAME ERRORS

When it came to fighting Kado Thorne in Creative Royale, his AI behavior had a bug. He couldn't use his Vampiric Health Drain ability. This caused him to just stand there and only attack if you got close enough. This bug occurred because boss special abilities do not work in Creative Royale.

SITTING POSTURE DEPENDING ON GENDER

In the real world, sitting positions are usually an unconscious, comfortable affair. In Fortnite, however, even the seemingly simple "Have a seat" Emote has been given a dose of attention to detail. You may have noticed that this emote has different variations for male and female outfits. For the male characters, we see the typical casual sitting left leg horizontal on the right leg, hands resting on knees and shins. The ladies, on the other hand, sit in a more elegant way, with their legs crossed and their hands resting on top of each other.

USER FIGURES AT A GLANCE

Fortnite is taking the world by storm. In just 6 years, the battle royale game has gone from a niche product to a global phenomenon. With a staggering 500 million players in March 2023, Fortnite has broken the half-a-billion barrier! By comparison, in May 2021 there were "only" 400 million players. This means that 100 million new Fortnite fans have been added in less than 2 years.

18+

OVER 60% OF FORTNITE PLAYERS ARE BETWEEN 18 AND 24 YEARS OLD. ALTHOUGH MANY YOUNGER USERS CHANGE THEIR AGE TO GAIN ACCESS TO FORTNITE, THE PERCENTAGE IS CALCULATED BASED ON THE DATE OF BIRTH GIVEN AT REGISTRATION. FORTNITE IS THEREFORE NOT ONLY ATTRACTIVE TO YOUNGER PLAYERS, BUT YOUNG ADULTS ALSO APPRECIATE THE GAME.

BACK TO THE ROOTS

Do you remember the good old days when *Fortnite* was still young and fresh? The OG map, the first attempts at building... For many, it was a dream that suddenly came true in November 2023! Epic's OG season took millions of *Fortnite* players on a journey back in time to the popular map of the first chapter. The campaign was a complete success: the mixture of nostalgia, fresh content and the return of the legendary map resulted in an incredible increase in players. Almost 1.5 billion game hours were recorded in *Fortnite* on Xbox and PlayStation in November - an increase of 146 percent compared to the previous month.

SUMMIT CLIMBER OR UNDERCOVER AGENT

Just as in real life you can draw conclusions about possible military service from uniforms or insignia, the Summit Striker Outfit also provides clues. The patch on the left-hand side could indicate that he is a member of the US Air Force, perhaps even with the rank of non-commissioned officer. His rucksack is also strongly reminiscent of military equipment.

KADO'S CABINET OF CURIOSITIES

Have you ever wondered what Kado Thorne does in his spare time? Well, there's a little secret you might not know yet: Cloistered Castle on Helios might be his personal museum! Why, you ask? Well, it seems he has a thing for collecting items from his past adventures. Imagine stumbling across Kado Thorne's bed and portrait from the Eclipse while wandering the halls. Or maybe you'll spot the Oathbound swords and shield hanging on the wall. There are even household items from the River Guard, lanterns from MEGA City, the arcade from the Peace Syndicate, vases from the Ancients, containers from the Explorers and bowling balls from Faulty Splits! It's almost as if Kado Thorne is trying to take a little piece of every world he's visited back home with him. Who knows, maybe he's planning a big housewarming party once his collection is complete. Until then, Cloistered Castle remains his very personal, somewhat bizarre museum.

THE BALL THAT STARTED IT ALL

Do you remember the early days, when the "Hookshot" toy was still a thing of the future? Back then, when the Item Shop was still in its infancy, there was already a very special object of desire: the football, also known in-game as "Pigskin." A simple ball, but it was the very first toy ever offered in the store.

BRUTUS BETRAYAL

Betrayal stabs deeper than a dagger, even in the world of Fortnite. So it's no wonder that Brutus is called a traitor by Jules during an in-game encounter because he has turned his back on SHADOW. Doesn't that remind you of the scene from the movie "Julius Caesar," where Marcus Brutus turns against Julius? And as if that wasn't enough, Brutus wears his GHOST uniform in the story trailer for Chapter 2: Season 3, which finally confirms his change of faction.

SO IS FORTNITE A MAN'S GAME?

In *Fortnite*, the boys rule - almost 90% of players are male. This is much higher than the proportion of women in gaming in general, which is around 45%. It seems that girls tend to use their smartphones for *Fortnite*, while guys prefer to play on consoles or PCs.

13

BUILDING AND FIGHTING FOR OVER A DECADE

Nowadays, in 2024, most gamers have probably heard of *Fortnite*. But did you know that the history of *Fortnite* goes back much further than you might think? In fact, the developers at Epic Games started developing the game back in 2011. Back then, *Fortnite* wasn't what we know it as today. There was no huge island where you competed against other players, no crazy dances and no fancy outfits. But the basic idea that you could build something in the game and then fight against others was already there. Were you already in the world then?

A HIT ON TIKTOK

Fortnite is the clear market leader in the area of gaming content on TikTok. With 2.9 billion views in 2023, it clearly outperforms the competition. GTA V follows in second place with 2.8 billion views, while Roblox (1.8 billion) and Minecraft (1.4 billion) are in third and fourth place.

WINNER WINNER CHICKEN DINNER

There are records in *Fortnite* that seem unattainable even for the most experienced players. One of them is OnlyGuyLeft's incredible solo win streak. Between November 18 and December 2, 2021, he achieved the almost impossible: 94 consecutive wins in solo mode. While even a few wins in a row are considered a success, this streak is a true feat that may even remain unmatched forever.

BUS DRIVER FAN CLUB

Did you know that you could thank the driver of the Battle Bus? You can show your appreciation by pressing the emote button. Your thanks will even be displayed in the Elimination Feed for all other players to see. Why does this feature even exist? Well, it was added as a result of a petition calling for this very feature.

GLITCH IN THE SYSTEM, GLIDER IN THE LOCKER

You may have the glider „Arcana" in your locker without having spent a single V-Buck on it. That's because Epic Games gave it away for free to all players after the Nexus event in May 2019. The reason for this was a technical error that prevented the event from starting after the countdown. As compensation, all players received the glider and those who had already purchased it received 1,200 V-Bucks back.

PYRAMID IN RECORD TIME

An important success factor in Fortnite is the ability to build quickly and precisely. Those who master this art have a decisive advantage over their opponents. A Swedish player has taken building in Fortnite to a new level and set a record with his extraordinary achievement that would make even experienced builders in the real world green with envy. He erected a three-story pyramid in just 56.90 seconds, a masterpiece of construction that is truly remarkable considering the short time available and the virtual environment.

THE FISH TO THE LEGENDARY ASSAULT RIFLE

If you grab the special Midas flopper fish, you will automatically receive a legendary assault rifle, i.e. the most powerful version of this weapon. It doesn't matter whether you already have an assault rifle. However, Midas floppers are quite rare, so you have to be attentive and patient when fishing.

REALISTIC MY ASS

Have you ever wondered whether the weapons in *Fortnite* really resemble their real-world counterparts? The assault rifle, for example, is based on the American M4 Carbine, but has a few inaccuracies: The front sight is mounted upside down and the receiver is missing important parts such as the dust cover and the locking aid.

SHELL GOES GAMING

Shell, a leading global oil and gas company, tried to win the hearts of young gamers in 2023 with a specially designed world in *Fortnite*. But instead of enthusiasm, the company was met with a storm of indignation. Gamers and environmental activists accused Shell of greenwashing and criticized the collaboration with well-known streamers and influencers who shared the virtual world with millions of followers.In particular, the fact that players in the virtual world are encouraged to fill up their cars with Shell's premium fuel V-Power NiTRO+ has been met with criticism. Many see this as a clumsy attempt to trivialize environmentally harmful products and attract young people to the brand.

LOADING SCREEN SECRET

Did you know that the B.R.U.T.E. Navigator outfit was originally planned with a completely different look? Imagine if the armor had been silver instead of black, with bright blue accents. And that's not all: this original armor had no connection to the B.R.U.T.E. mech. Although these early designs are still dormant in the game files, they have been overlaid by the final textures. But wait, there is one exception: In the B.R.U.T.E. Squad loading screen, this original silver armor is actually worn.

WHERE HUSKS STILL SCREAMED LIKE TEENAGERS

AHH...

In early versions of *Fortnite*, the Husks had significantly lighter skin and emitted shrill, high-pitched screams. Instead of disappearing in the familiar purple cloud, they ended in a skeletal explosion followed by a blood-red pool on the ground. This depiction was later changed to make the game experience less disturbing.

OWN MONOPOLY

Did you know that you can't just dive into the world of battle royale virtually? There is a special version of the classic board game „Monopoly" in which you don't fight for streets and train stations, but for well-known locations from the game. Instead of building houses and hotels, you build walls and chests to defeat your opponents.

CONTROLLER WITH VITAMIN B(ANANA)

Want to take your *Fortnite* look to the next level and stand out from the crowd? PowerA has just the thing for you: a brand-new collection of exclusive controllers and accessories straight from the colorful world of *Fortnite*. For all Nintendo Switch fans, there is a controller that not only impresses with its functions, but is also a real eye-catcher. It features the design of Peely, the iconic banana from *Fortnite*. Imagine holding a bright yellow banana in your hands as you fend off your opponents - a truly hilarious sight! But that's not all: the collection also includes a matching case and headphones in the Peely design, so you can match your entire gaming look to *Fortnite*.

THE LEGEND OF THE MOST DAMAGING WEAPON IN FORTNITE

Have you noticed that there aren't as many really powerful weapons in *Fortnite* that can completely change the gameplay? It used to be different. Before 2020, for example, there was the Heavy Sniper Rifle, an ultra-rare weapon that terrified every *Fortnite* player. With a single shot, you could inflict 157 points of damage on your opponent - more than enough to take out even the strongest players. But that wasn't all: the Heavy Sniper also had an environmental damage rating of 1100. Entire buildings could be razed to the ground in seconds with this weapon.

DESOLATE MOOD

In the first drafts of Fortnite, things were much darker. With gruesome monsters and a bleak environment inspired by "Gears of War" and "Unreal," the game seemed rather depressing. However, this mood was too negative for the developers in the long run. To make Fortnite more playable and appealing, they opted for a more cartoonish style that was more inviting.

THE PERENNIAL FAVORITE

Fortnite currently has an average of 221 million players every month. During the worst of the COVID-19 pandemic, the game became even more popular because many people had to stay at home. Although the pandemic is over, more than 220 million people are still playing *Fortnite* today. It's just a lot of fun!

BEING GOOD PAYS OFF

Do you know the Krampus outfit? The scary costume has its origins in German legends. While Santa Claus hands out presents on the night of 24th to 25th December, Krampus makes his grand entrance on 5th December albeit with far fewer presents and all the more fear and terror. In German folklore, the Krampus is a terrifying demon with horns, a goatee, and a furry coat. He accompanies Santa Claus on his way and punishes disobedient children with rods and chains. In some regions of Germany, disguised Krampuses even go from house to house and scare the children.

HAPPY HOUR FOR PREDATORS

Think you know all the tricks in *Fortnite*? Then wait until you hear how you can use the meat supply to keep wild animals at bay. If you suddenly hear a raptor growling in-game and see it coming towards you, you can throw it a piece of meat to distract it. What will happen? In *Fortnite*, raptors and wolves actually eat all the meat they find on the ground to heal their HP. Before they attack you or other animals, they even prefer to eat their fill first. This can give you a decisive advantage in tricky situations! So remember: meat is your friend when it comes to appeasing wild animals in *Fortnite*.

10 A SUPERSTAR CONQUERS NEW WORLDS

You know Neymar Jr. as a soccer superstar who plays entire defensive lines dizzy with his dribbling. But did you know that he has also caused a sensation in another arena - without a ball or turf? In April 2021, he made history when he became the first footballer ever to be immortalized as a playable character in *Fortnite*.

SHORT AND SWEET

The AC/DC Pickaxe is not only a cool collector's item but also a tribute to the legendary rock band AC/DC and their energetic live shows.

Until Chapter 5, all Battle Royale maps were named after Greek deities beginning with the letter "A."

The very first season of *Fortnite* Battle Royale ran from September to December 2017.

Of all the bosses in *Fortnite*, Darth Vader has the fewest voice lines, beating even Iron Man.

The first vehicle in *Fortnite* was the Ferrari 296 GTB.

SHORT AND SWEET

Every year on *Fortnite*'s birthday, the Battle Bus decorates itself with confetti, balloons and the number of its special day.

Helios, the codename for the Fortnite Battle Royale map introduced in Chapter 5, breaks with the trend of naming the map after Greek deities that begin with "A."

Epic has added temporary warnings on *Fortnite* loading screens to discourage students from playing the game during class.

The "Hot Marat" emote appears in a scene from the 2019 comedy "Chaos on the Net."

JOHN WICK'S WILD SHOTGUN

The combat shotgun in Fortnite has an unexpected connection to the world of cinema; it is a precise replica of the Italian Benelli M2 Super 90 shotgun. This weapon gained particular popularity through its use in the movie "John Wick: Chapter 3 Parabellum." The introduction of the combat shotgun in Fortnite specifically coincided with the release of the movie. The reloading animations of the combat shotgun in the game are also closely based on John Wick's characteristic moves in the movie.

FROM COMICS TO CHAOS

Deadpool, the unpredictable antihero with the loose mouth, is not only known for his chaotic actions, but also for his groundbreaking role in *Fortnite*. He was the very first co-op boss to ever appear in Battle Royale mode, ushering in a new era of collaboration between *Fortnite* and other franchises. As if that wasn't enough, he was also the first Marvel character to break into the *Fortnite* world, opening the door for numerous other superheroes and villains from the Marvel Universe.

WELDING WAS YESTERDAY

Before the invention of the repair torch, gamers had to come up with a lot of ideas to get wrecked cars and trucks back in shape. Bonfires were the only way to repair dents and scratches. This could sometimes be really nerve-wracking in hectic battles because you had to make a quick getaway. The repair torch made repairs child's play. Simply spray it on and bang, the vehicle shines again. Unfortunately, this was later removed from the game.

PIGS WITH ALIEN SLIME

Be careful when you are out and about in the woods. There are special wild boars lurking there that are infested with alien parasites and have changed their appearance as a result. If you come across one, take special care not to get hit by its slime, as it will slowly drain your health. If you strike down a parasite wild boar, the parasite will pass on to you.

WHAT ARE THESE COOL MOVES?

Imagine sneaking up to an enemy base in *Fortnite*, full of tension and concentration. But suddenly you see an imposing boss who seems to have lost his mind. In the middle of the room, he's making wild dance moves. Don't panic, he's not just celebrating his victory, he's bugged. When AI-controlled characters such as guards or bosses get stuck and their pathfinding system stops working, they start dancing until the bug is fixed. And the best part? The dance animations are often actually the emotes you can use yourself in the game. It's a fun sight to see a fearsome boss groove to disco fever or crazy robot moves.

MYSTERIOUS MISSION OBJECTIVES

In some *Fortnite* Save the World missions, especially those where you have to collect resources, so-called „anomalies" can appear as part of the mission objectives. These anomalies look like purple rocks that you must destroy to find four crystals. Collect all the crystals to get BluGlo.

THE HIGHEST EARNING FORTNITE BATTLE ROYALE ESPORTS PLAYER

Kyle Giersdorf aka „Bugha" from the USA has established himself as one of the highest earning players thanks to his success in *Fortnite* Battle Royale eSports tournaments. By 2024, he had won a total of over 3 million euros in prize money. He owes the majority of this impressive sum to his historic victory at the *Fortnite* World Cup Finals 2019 in the solo category. This triumph at the age of just 16 catapulted Bugha to fame virtually overnight.

PANDORA'S BOX COULDN'T WAIT

In Chapter 5: Season 1, the Pandora's Box Opening event was overshadowed by an unexpected glitch. Shortly before the end of the event, in which players were supposed to free a Pandora's Box in order to unlock new content, the box opened prematurely for some players. Although the event was still running, it was practically all over.

INSPIRATION FROM THE FAR EAST

Both *Fortnite* Battle Royale and PUBG were inspired by the Japanese film „Battle Royale". In this bleak scenario, students are abandoned on an island and have to compete against each other in a merciless fight for survival until there is only one winner left. The film is based on the 1999 novel of the same name by Japanese author Koushun Takami and, with its relentless depiction of violence and coercion, shaped the battle royale genre as we know it today.

FORTNITE STATUS ICON

The „Crowning Achievement" Emote is not static, but changes with the number of victories. While players without crowns can use the emote but are displayed without a crown, players with 1 to 9 victories receive a simple crown on the pillow. From 10 victories, a second head is added to the crown and from 20 victories, the emote becomes even more magnificent with a third head on the crown and red gemstones.

PETER'S GENUFLECTION

Peter Griffin, the character known from Family Guy, is not only known for his sayings, but also for his unique animation when he is defeated. After his defeat, he winces in pain while sitting on his knee, a reference to a famous gag from the episode "Wasted Talent." This makes him the second boss after Darth Vader to have such a special animation.

SHOTGUN WITH A REAL BITE

You may already be a real *Fortnite* gun expert, but did you know that the Nightclaw is a tribute to the American Mossberg Maverick 88? Just like its real-life counterpart, you can fold up the stock of the Nightclaw to make it more compact. But beware, the inscription „BOSSMERG 12" under the ejection port is not real, but a witty allusion to the names of real gun manufacturers. And here's the trick: the Nightclaw, the Panther and the Longarm Enforcer are basically the same weapon, just with different attachments.

IT WAS TIME TO SAY GOODBYE

Despite the initial euphoria, Fortnite had to give in to enormous pressure from the Chinese government authorities after a relatively short period of operation: new, restrictive regulations and limitations for online games made the continued operation of Fortnite on the Chinese market simply unfeasible. The hoped-for collaboration between Epic Games and Tencent turned out to be a disappointment. In October 2021, Tencent announced the inevitable end of the Chinese version of Fortnite. Just one month later, on November 15, 2021, this announcement became a reality: the servers for the Chinese version were permanently shut down and new players could no longer register.

GLOBAL PHENOMENON

With 21% of players, the United States has the largest *Fortnite* community. That equates to a whopping 108 million players! Russia follows in second place with a share of around 8% and around 38 million enthusiastic gamers. But *Fortnite*'s popularity knows no bounds! Players from all corners of the world immerse themselves in the colorful world of the game.

NETWORK CHAOS WITH SPIDEY FANS

On November 18, 2023, the time had finally come: Spider-Man's web shooters were introduced to *Fortnite*. Players rushed to try out the new gadgets, but the servers couldn't cope with the rush. Many had login problems and Epic Games had to deactivate the net shooters after less than an hour - causing disappointment and chaos among fans. Fortunately, however, errors were quickly rectified and the networkers provided plenty of action when they returned.

MIDAS INTENTIONS

Midas, the infamous leader of SHADOW, may not have had the best of intentions when he tried to control the storm. Contrary to popular belief, he didn't want to destroy the storm to save the loopers, but only for his own gain. Even though Midas Rex is described in Epic Games' blog posts as someone with "best intentions," this is probably just a euphemism to say that he didn't intentionally want to flood the island. His true motives, however, remain shrouded in mystery.

FORTNITE FEVER

Did you know that Netflix had 125 million streaming subscribers worldwide in the first quarter of 2018? Impressive, isn't it? But what's even more amazing is that *Fortnite* reached the same number of registered players in less than a year after its release. And not only that, over 40 million people play the game at least once a month. Crazy, right?

FORTNITE SECURITY CHECK

Have you ever wondered how safe *Fortnite* is? A cybersecurity organization investigated just that and rated the game 703 out of 950 in terms of security. Furthermore, another company reported that they were able to detect 53,000 cases of fraud on *Fortnite*. Interestingly, 86% of these scams took place via social media platforms, while 11% were via fake web domains and 2% via YouTube. Tip: So it's important to be vigilant when playing *Fortnite*, especially when engaging with other players online. Never give out your personal details or account information and don't click on suspicious links or attachments.

IN FORTNITE, A MONUMENT WAS ERECTED IN 2018 IN HONOR OF MUSELK'S TRAGICALLY FAILED RESCUE ATTEMPT FOR HIS TEAMMATE CHAPPADOODLE. MUSELK ATTEMPTED TO RESCUE CHAPPADOODLE WITH A GOLF CART THAT WAS OUTSIDE THE BUILDABLE ZONE OF THE MAP. HOWEVER, THE ATTEMPT ENDED FATALLY FOR BOTH PLAYERS. DESPITE THE TRAGIC OUTCOME, EPIC GAMES HONORED MUSELK'S SELFLESS ACT WITH A MEMORIAL.

MOST VIEWED FORTNITE VIDEO

The most popular *Fortnite* video on YouTube is „The *Fortnite* Rap Battle | #NerdOut ft Ninja, CDNThe3rd, Dakotaz, H2O Delirious & More by NerdOut!" from 2018. The video presents a funny *Fortnite* rap with special guests, accompanied by game scenes from *Fortnite* from 2017. As of May 2024, it has reached 136 million views.

BIG BANG EVENT BLAST SERVER

Over 10 million players wanted to see the storyline event "The Big Bang" in Fortnite, which led to server problems so severe that some players had to queue for over an hour, while others couldn't even get into the game. Epic Games repeated the event twice to give all players a chance to see it, but had to cancel the second iteration due to ongoing server issues. Only the third performance went smoothly.

FORTNITE FEVER WITH REAL HITS

Swap the controller for a real blaster. At Laser Mayhem in Essex, UK, you can recreate the virtual *Fortnite* experience in real life. On a huge terrain modeled after the game's iconic locations, you can team up with friends, search for rivals and fight for victory. Not only do you have to keep an eye on your opponents, but you also have to escape the gathering storm. What are you waiting for?

Why don't you show off your skills in real life ;)

CRIT WITH THE STAR WAND

The Star Wand and AC/DC Pickaxe had a bug that caused them to deal 56 damage on every attack, with a 1.5x headshot bonus. This was quickly fixed, but it was unusual as it was the only time this weapon could deal critical damage to players.

PURPLE MOOD IN LOOT LAKE

In the fifth Fortnite season, a strange, purple-colored cube called "Kevin" appeared at Loot Lake. What looked harmless at first was actually a creature from another world with an evil plan: to destroy the island! The cube, Kevin, was not only creepy but also dangerous. Any player who touched him immediately lost many life points. Even cars were simply crushed by him.

FROM THE APOCALYPSE TO THE BATTLE ROYALE GIANT

Fortnite was not originally intended to be a battle royale shooter. The first game mode in *Fortnite* in 2017 was called Save the World and placed players in a post-apocalyptic world where they had to fight monstrous creatures. Instead of competing against each other in Battle Royale, players built fortresses together and defended them with weapons. It was only later that the popular battle royale mode was added, making *Fortnite* the worldwide phenomenon it is today.

FORTNITE JENGA

Imagine being in Fortnite and seeing players wildly stacking the "Spiky Stadium" item on top of each other. This was only possible because of a wacky glitch where you could throw the stadium and, so to speak, grab it onto yourself. The stadium got higher and higher until it suddenly disappeared from the game. It was then invisible and full of bugs. The glitch was quickly fixed, but it was a cool, unpredictable experience for everyone who was there.

The "Spiky Stadium" was a special item in *Fortnite* that could be used in the "Playground" mode. It was a large, portable stadium that players could place. The highlight of this stadium was the spiked traps and bouncers scattered around the walls and interior. Unfortunately, the item was removed from the game in Season 7.

THE BOSS WHO SQUEEZES YOU

Doctor Doom is not only a popular boss but the first to be made bigger than the normal players. This change was introduced before the standardization in Chapter 3 Season 2 and made him a unique opponent. Interestingly, Doctor Doom was also the only boss of this size to have the shakedown option, which allowed players to gain information on other enemies. The Cube Assassin, another large character, does not count here as she could only be brought down by a glitch.

NOSTALGIA WAVE

At the beginning of November 2023, *Fortnite* set a new record to date with 44.7 million players active in the Battle Royale world for 102 million hours. At the same time, there were up to 6 million players on the servers. The four-week special season *Fortnite* OG, which was launched shortly beforehand, was responsible for this onslaught. This season takes players back to the roots of the battle royale and evokes pure nostalgia with the original map from 2017 and legendary locations such as Tilted Towers and Greasy Grove.

WITH BUBBLES INTO STRATOSPHERE

Imagine you have the power to bend the laws of physics! With the bubble effect ability, this becomes possible. It's not just there to let you glide gently through the air, but also provides some unexpected and funny moments. For example, what happens when you ac-tivate the bubble effect and the low-gravity effect is active at the same time? Quite simply, you float around like an astronaut. It is also possible to activate the low-gravity effect while holding a chicken. And if you've always wanted to make a really long jump, combine the bubble effect with a jump from a great height. You'll be amazed at how far you can fly! But that's not all! If you combine the bubble effect with a saucer, you can hurl other players to unimagined distances.

SMALL SIZE, BIG EGO

Mini-bosses can be pretty mean. Sometimes they have several special abilities at the same time, which can make the fight very difficult for you. Imagine a mini-boss can almost destroy your buildings in one hit and increase your damage with each hit at the same time. Or he can blow you up with every shot so that you can barely aim. It's hard to keep calm.

SHORT AND SWEET

The name of the 928 Axes harvesting tool is a possible allusion to Earth-928 from Marvel Comics, the home of Spider-Man 2099.

The code name of the boss "Huntmaster Saber" is "Thunder Meow."

The code name of the boss "Glyph Master Raz" is "TinyBalloon."

The characters Beef Boss and Tomato Head are enemies.

If you use the Symbol of Peace emote with the All Might outfit in the game, a unique laughter animation is performed.

CAT-AND-MOUSE GAME

Abductors are like nasty surprises. They suddenly appear, grab you and disappear just as quickly. You never know when and where they will appear and they never stay in one place for long. They are real ghosts who just want to cause trouble. So always be on your guard, because the kidnappers could turn your game upside down at any time!

FLYING HIGH WITH STYLE

Are you looking for a *Fortnite* outfit that not everyone has? Then the Aerial Assault Trooper from Spitfire is exactly what you need to add the finishing touch to your outfit. It is not only an eye-catcher, but also a sign of your exclusive sense of style. Many players consider it a real rarity, as it was only available in the item store for a short time and has never appeared again since.

EPIC GAMES VS. CHEATERS

In the fight for fair playing conditions in Fortnite, developer Epic Games is taking rigorous action against cheaters. The company does not even shy away from lawsuits against minors, as a case from 2017 shows, in which a 14-year-old was sued for using cheats. Epic Games uses a multi-pronged system to combat cheating in Fortnite. In addition to a robust anti-cheat system that automatically detects and blocks cheaters, game observers are also used to actively search for conspicuous behavior in live tournaments. Epic Games is particularly targeting users of cheat websites and providers of "aimbot" software, which gives players an unfair advantage in battle. Epic Games justifies its crackdown with violations of the end user license agreement and copyright infringements. Although cheating in Fortnite has been made more difficult by Epic Games' measures, it remains a challenge, especially in competitive play. However, the risks for cheaters are high, as Epic Games is taking consistent action against cheating and does not rule out legal action in the future.

SHORT AND SWEET

The development of the Battle Royale mode only took about two months.

With an average of 6 to 10 hours of game time per week, *Fortnite* takes over the free time of many players. That's 91 to 152 full days a year if you really play every day.

Chapter 4: Season 4 has the least number of map changes, only three in total.

Is there an island where you can compete in a bot battle as Angela Merkel and Olaf Scholz? In "Politician Battle: Merkel vs. Scholz" by yasicreeper, 16 players fight for political dominance.

SHORT AND SWEET

Fortnite drew inspiration for the design of its characters and environments from the works of Pixar and Looney Tunes, among others.

Jack Skellington, the Pumpkin King from Tim Burton's "The Nightmare Before Christmas," holds a special record: he is the first outfit in Fortnite from the Walt Disney Company to be based on an animated character.

The "Cobra Coin" Backbling pays homage to the Netflix series "Cobra Kai."

The Arroyo Pack was the first Legendary Free Pass item in *Fortnite*.

Epilogue

Congratulations, reader! You've fought your way through an epic collection of useless Fortnite knowledge and emerged victorious! In this book, you've discovered treasures that would surprise even the most seasoned Battle Royale veteran.

Sometimes it's the little details that make the game memorable: the secret dances of the NPCs, the hidden Easter Eggs, or the stories behind the skins.

And while this knowledge might not get you the epic win, it's a great way to show off, right? Challenge your squadmates by impressing them with your newfound Fortnite expertise, whether you're a master builder who builds faster than your shadow twitches or you've just attempted your first skydive stay curious!

There's always something new to discover, both in the ever-changing world of Fortnite and in real life. So, grab your harvesting tool and jump into the next match! The next adventure is already waiting for you!

1. Edition

Johannes Schwegler und Oliver Hagel GbR
c/o Block Services
Stuttgarter Str. 106
70736 Fellbach
Deutschland

Printed in Great Britain
by Amazon

54565945R00079